AERIAL APES

AERIAL APES

GIBBONS OF ASIA

Geza Teleki   Lori Baldwin   Meredith Rucks

COWARD, McCANN & GEOGHEGAN, INC.
NEW YORK

For *SHIRLEY and ARDITH*
Guardians of wild gibbons

ACKNOWLEDGMENTS

We are indebted to the arboreal gibbons who tolerated their terrestrial human cousins—even in the most trying times of captivity. And we are grateful to our editor, Susan Shapiro, for improving upon this book.

All photographs were taken by Geza Teleki and Lori Baldwin

Text copyright © 1979 by Geza Teleki, Lori Baldwin, and
Meredith Rucks
Photographs copyright © 1979 by Geza Teleki and Lori Baldwin

Library of Congress Cataloging in Publication Data

Teleki, Geza   Aerial apes

SUMMARY: Photographs and text document the world of an Asian gibbon in its treetop environment.

1. Gibbons—Juvenile literature.   2. Mammals—Asia—Juvenile
literature.   [1. Gibbons]
I. Baldwin, Lori, joint author.   II. Rucks, Meredith, joint
author.   III. Title.
QL737.P96T43   599'.882   78-10721   ISBN 0-698-20477-8

Book design by Kathleen Westray   Printed in the U.S.A.

The display and text type are set in Bembo.
The book was printed by offset at Rae Lithographers.

Millions of years ago the ancestors of wild gibbons lived in vast forests stretching across Europe, Africa, and Asia. Today gibbons live only in the more remote forests of Asia, from southern China down to the islands of Sumatra, Java, and Borneo.

The white-handed gibbons (*Hylobates lar*) shown in this book are but one of 7 different kinds, or species, and can be found mainly in Thailand and Malaya. They are almost entirely arboreal, living high above the ground in lush, tropical rain forests and cool mountain woodlands. Where there are no trees, there are also no gibbons.

This species can be identified by a white face ring, white hands, and white feet. These features stand out because the body hair is normally black or buff, although some gibbons may be silver gray or even pure white. The body hair is dense and woolly, thicker than that of any other primate: up to 13,125 very fine hairs can grow from 1 square inch of skin.

Gibbons have other unusual traits. They use very long and sinewy arms to sway and swing from tree to tree, and slender hands as hooks for hanging on branches and vines. Even when the hands are relaxed, special tendons and muscles arch the fingers so the gibbons do not lose their grip. During rare moments on the ground, they will hold tightly onto low branches for security. Gibbons' bones are light, like those of birds, and their bodies are very slim. Adults weigh less than 15 pounds and barely reach 3 feet from head to heel when standing upright.

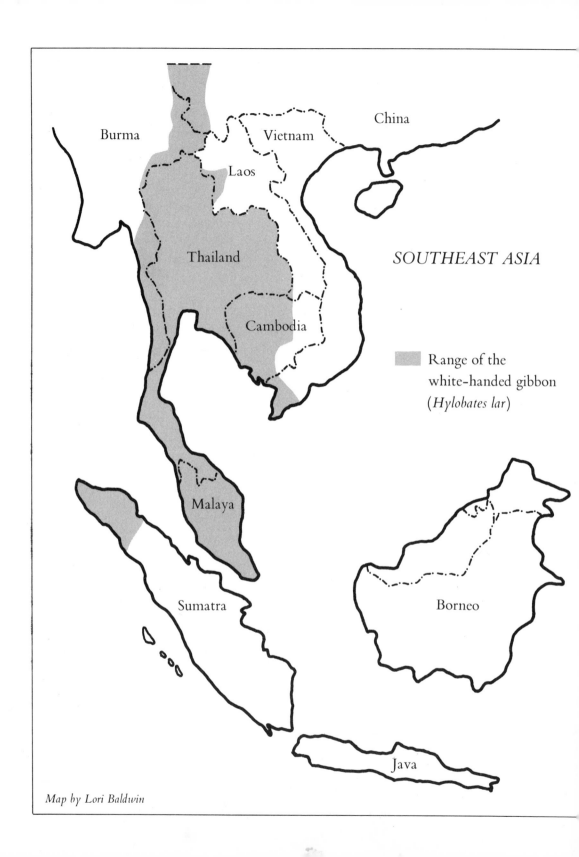

China

Burma

Vietnam

Laos

SOUTHEAST ASIA

Thailand

Cambodia

Range of the
white-handed gibbon
(*Hylobates lar*)

Malaya

Sumatra

Borneo

Java

Map by Lori Baldwin

Gibbons are classified as apes, not monkeys, in part because they have no tails. But gibbons are sometimes called Lesser Apes because they are so much smaller than the three Great Apes: chimpanzees, gorillas, and orangutans. Supple and strong, gibbons are master aerial acrobats, treetop trapeze artists who can twist and turn, swoop and soar through the high forest canopy.

Gibbons live in small family groups of no more than 5 members: a father and a mother, and up to 3 youngsters of different ages. Each gibbon family uses a territory which may reach 100 acres in size and defends this forest area against all gibbon strangers. Every young gibbon must eventually leave home to find a mate and to settle a new territory where the family then lives for 20 or more years.

Family members travel, feed, and sleep together. Getting up at dawn, they spend most of the day foraging and feeding on fruits and leaves, buds and flowers. Insects and bird eggs are also eaten on occasion. Gibbons get most of their water from juicy plants, but sometimes they drop to the ground for cool drinks at pools or streams. There are many rest stops during the day, when adults can groom, running lips and fingers through one another's hair to remove bits of dirt or flakes of dry skin, and youngsters can play, chasing and wrestling while suspended in the air. Gibbons settle down for the night in tall trees, well before sunset. They do not build nests, but simply wrap around or wedge into spreading branches to keep from falling while asleep.

Because gibbons live in such dense forest terrain, so high above the ground, they are very difficult to study in their Asian homeland. Our observations and photographs were made in Bermuda, where several gibbons had been released on a small, uninhabited island for scientific study.

Soaring high, a graceful gibbon dives through the air, tracing a smooth curve across the sky. With arms outstretched and legs bent, a gibbon can easily span 30 feet of space in one leap.

As they travel along familiar treetop trails in upward leaps and downward jumps, gibbons use hands as feet or feet as hands. Sharp eyesight and strong, supple limbs give split-second timing and sure balance for aerial acrobatics at speeds up to 40 miles per hour.

A buff gibbon rests, alert to all sounds and sights in the surrounding foliage. Liquid black eyes match a dark face framed by white whiskers.

A black gibbon, hair blown by the wind, glances backward, flashing a white face ring. The hair is fantastically fine yet dense. The tips of the ears can just be seen.

Even in the downpour of a sudden storm the woolly hair does not soak through to the skin. When the sun comes out again, the gibbon is dry in no time at all.

A dark shadow springs from a tree like a black arrow shot from a bow. The gibbon lands, then hangs effortlessly, swaying in a gentle breeze.

High above ground or low, heads up or down, two gibbons play in a tangle of locked limbs.

Even when they rest or forage, gibbons bend like supple
reeds into as many shapes as the branches on the trees.

The gibbon is the most spectacular aerialist in the arboreal world. Here, arms held apart for balance, feet gripping a branch, a buff gibbon prepares…

to launch into the air...

to leap...

and alight...

and sometimes fall all the way down to the ground,
where he sprawls on his behind.

But a fall is rarely dangerous for the nimble gibbon, though he whoops loudly to show his wide-eyed surprise.

Soon he is running along the grassy ground
to quickly reach a stand of trees

and scramble up a slender sapling, where he stops near the
top and hangs, ready to shoot into space once again.

Gibbons are so active that they must spend many short spans of time—adding up to 5 or 6 hours each day—picking tasty leaves and fruits. Reaching and searching with deft fingers, they also hunt for insects under tree bark and inside leaf clusters.

An hour or two before the sun sets, a drowsy gibbon pauses to gaze at other gibbons settling into nearby trees.

Even in sleep, the gibbon is an aerial ape, balanced on a branch while curled in a fluffy heap.

AFTERWORD

A captive gibbon is not a complete gibbon. Like a fish in the water or a bird in flight, a gibbon in his treetop home has a majestic presence that cannot be seen anywhere else. Take away the water, the wind, or the tree, break the natural bonds between animals and their worlds, and much of that splendor will vanish.

Although we studied gibbons in captivity, we feel there is no reasonable excuse for removing them from the wilderness. And we hope our book carries that message to others who might think that gibbons are gibbons wherever they have been placed by humans.

02